A CROSSROADS IN TIME

Edited by

Heather Killingray

First published in Great Britain in 2003 by
POETRY NOW
Remus House,
Coltsfoot Drive,
Peterborough, PE2 9JX
Telephone (01733) 898101
Fax (01733) 313524

HB ISBN 0 75434 433 9
SB ISBN 0 75434 434 7

FOREWORD

Although we are a nation of poets we are accused of not reading poetry, or buying poetry books. After many years of listening to the incessant gripes of poetry publishers, I can only assume that the books they publish, in general, are books that most people do not want to read.

Poetry should not be obscure, introverted, and as cryptic as a crossword puzzle: it is the poet's duty to reach out and embrace the world.

The world owes the poet nothing and we should not be expected to dig and delve into a rambling discourse searching for some inner meaning.

The reason we write poetry (and almost all of us do) is because we want to communicate: an ideal; an idea; or a specific feeling. Poetry is as essential in communication, as a letter; a radio; a telephone, and the main criterion for selecting the poems in this anthology is very simple: they communicate.

She Remembered
Written By:
Susan Carole Gash-Roberts
On Page 120.

CONTENTS

I WONDER . . .

I wonder what would happen if I tried
To comprehend your
Mind and even to
Appreciate
Just
Why

But tonight you're mine; that
Is all very fine.

Thanks to the wine.

Paula Puddephatt

THE TERRORS OF THE NIGHT

When darkness wraps around my world
And glimmer is the light of lights
Festooned around me high and low
Are creatures all devoid of souls
In hanging form or flying near
They creak and crack and moan like wind
I listen hard to find their place
But they assail me from all sides
With eyes agog and straining ears
I cannot put a pin to them
A whisper here a footfall there
I seem embraced within their beings
Tormentors of these darkened hours
Those guardians of the black mystique
Begone, desert me, peace I crave
But deafened ears ignore my pleas
Alone I lie, without an aid
The only one on earth awake
For all the rest are slumbering sound
Just me, a solitary soul is found.

Terence Stephen McNeela

VOICES

Clanging door
Shivering wall
Who will hear our silent call?

Day turns dark
The night draws near
Who cares about our silent fear?

Next in line
Brother lies
'Neath the blanket
Stares - wide eyes

Mother shouts
And father rages
We their prisoners
In our cages

Long night through
There is no rest
No one here to hug or bless

One more sunrise
One more day
Just the same as yesterday

There is no joy
There is no play
There is no love
There is no way
That we can be but children now
We learned that
Long ago
Somehow.

Lorraine M McLeod

THE YORKSHIRE DALES IN RAIN

We wandered through the drizzling rain
across vetch fields, up wooded hills,
and down to valleys once again.
We splashed ankle-deep through tumbling becks
while heavy clouds loured down from gun-grey skies,
and burst with spears of heavy rain
to drench us both with shivering cold and made
us hurry to a jutting cave.
We clasped our stone-cold hands and laid
our rough-hewn sticks against the rock.
Stamping our booted feet we laughed
with the freedom of the young and there
with faces lacrimose with streams of rain
we kissed and hugged, then laughed with joy again.
We were alone in a magic world awash
with green and bronze and grey
with water all around us on this wild, October day.
The pounding rain now sheeted less ferociously
so daringly, with youth's mad hearts we struggled forth,
and slipped in mud up to the knee!
Ahead of us, from towering hills fell thunderous
water with a mighty roar. In triple waterfalls
it gushed and crashed in pounding waves to stony pools
                                    too deep to see.
From hills all round rain rivulets to join the becks below.
Our world of water gave us breathless joy
and even through our runny eyes and dripping hair
we felt our cheeks and fingers glow.
Oh, it was cold and wet and dismally damp and grey
but we had spent a wild, enchanting day.

Betty M Irwin-Burton

MY BEST FRIEND

It's not just what you've done for me that makes me love you so.
It's all the joy of who you are the friend I've come to know.
And everything you do or say, means a lot to me in every way.
You are someone I can rely on, someone I can trust,
A shoulder to cry on when things go wrong.
You are always there when I need you most,
No matters what life throws at us?
Our lives through the years will always change,
But with a friend like you, our friendship will never end.

Carol Coker

HAND-WRITTEN

I write by hand,
I like the physical
feel of the pen
in my hand,
the touch of the paper,
the contact between
mind and hand.
I think if it was
good enough for
Dickens
it's good enough for me.
I write by hand.

Greig Linton

In Memoriam

Come sit with me a little while
As I do the things that must be done
As I take the dear things tenderly
And destroy them slowly, one by one.

Come give me cheer that this my task
Might not so sad and tragic seem
And with your presence give the room
A touch or two, perhaps a gleam
Of warmth and sunshine, that my heart
Shall not the coldness nor the hurt sustain.
A little while I ask that you should play this part
And when it's done no more we'll speak of it, we two
Except perhaps long days ahead
When memory is kinder still.

Pam Love

SAM

He knew, Sam
He sensed the absence
He'd heard it all over the years
The trivialities, incensed rows, intimate murmuring
The crying, laughing
Hopelessly devoted he'd been, unable to
Detach himself the final weeks
Even the bitch heavy in season didn't
Tempt him to stray
He stayed, he sat at the foot of the
Bed . . . devoted till the end
He knew, Sam
He knew time was running out
The bitch could wait
The bitch would be there tomorrow
She wouldn't. Sam knew.
He knew then, he knows now.
The empty chair, once forbidden to him.
Now he feels no need to grace it
With his presence
Is the bitch on heat?
He hasn't noticed
First time for everything so they say
He can't come to terms with the absence
Unnatural quite?
Who will walk him now?
And scold him for shedding his once
Beautiful groomed coat on her chair
Her chair . . . eternally.

S Lea-Morris

DEMENTIA

Illness has
come upon us
is it a dream
or is it true?

Vile and sarcastic
words break
into our souls.

Our mother has
uttered them.

Old and infirm
makes no odds

the words
have
been spoken
to a grieving
son and daughter.

Pam Bridgwater

DRIVING

Flack flack.
Not completely effective, are they?
Wipe the cold condensing
into smears to render vision
blemished and obscured,
see the world eyed misty.
Slap slap,
and from outside
a different, drowning,
deeper intermittent drum
beats to speed the pulse
with thoughts of breaking down;
imaginings of soaked waiting
for rescue
that could lead
in drenched intense nothingness
to personal breakdown.

Might make more sense
to call the lifeboat.

Let speeds drop
and home moves away
further than at fifty.
But if something minor
were to fall off,
(like a wheel),
better stop slow
than fast.
The mind is more adept at creating
disaster,
envisioning mayhem;
brings more vivid pictures
to failure
than it does to imaginings
of saved success.

'Get there, car,
that's all that's asked,
it's all you need do,
just get there.'

Slap slap,
flack flack,
slosh.
A bagful of chips
steaming alongside
wafts a smell
of tasty dryness
against tastebuds
as wet as the world.

Coda:
May the con-rods not connecting
Make the noise the mind's dissecting?
Drumming drowns the tappets tappeting
And exhausted pipes a-rattling.
Has a gaiter on the CVs
Got the dreaded heebie-jeebies?
Have the big-ends met each little,
Is the coolant boiled to spittle;
Do the wheel nuts clatter round
Inside the knave-plates - dreadful sound?

But once the journey's end is met
Who cares what the noise was yet?
Lock the car; avoid the drips,
In to get outside those chips.

Seán Jackson

THE WHITE CIRCLE

Rolling ropes of white
Circle the sandbanks,
Continue the white circle of your arm
Above my head
In the white crescent of the bay.
In this symphony of white and blue
Warm sand trickles to your arm
As my hand and Heaven touches you.

Richard Blomfield

IN THE BLINK OF AN EYE

We pass as shadows in the night,
As ships on the high sea.
We touch as waves caress the shore,
As the sun lays upon the sea.
You are a flicker of bright light,
A swirling mist of haze,
Brief as a rainbow in the rain,
A bolt of lightning in a storm.
We are just merely butterflies,
Flitting on the breeze.
Touching for a moment with our hearts
And flying on again.
We are but sunrays,
From behind a cloud,
A shadow from a bee.
We are a drop of dew upon the grass,
That soon will fly away.
You are a moonbeam in the darkness,
The slight blink of a small star,
Just a flicker before a cloud does form.
A slight thunderous rumble in the far off distance,
Or the dance of a firefly by night,
Under the stars' slight light.

Hannah Inglis

BENEATH THE CANOPY

Suddenly . . .
Vulnerability.
Savouring sensations of
Fear
And my neck throbs.
Eyes dart to every corner
Sniffing around for
Alien life
Or mutant form
Or shapely foreign figures.
Bring my knees up to my
Chest to save my toes.
Eyes hover like a one-winged
Firefly over the towering objects - still
Stabbing the air viciously.
In dark disgust they watch
Over my covered face.

Through the wall they see
And through their net I fall.

Joanne Bartlett

OH TO BE A CHILD AGAIN

Oh to be a child again,
And gamble o'er the hills.
To pick wild things,
And laugh and sing,
And wander where I will.

Oh to be a child again,
Irresponsible and free.
To have no work,
Except to learn,
All that interests me.

Oh to be a child again,
Unaware of harm or dread.
Snug, secure
And reassured,
Sleeping soundly in my bed.

Oh to be a child again,
Adulthood is no fun.
It's down to me,
Whate'er I'll be,
And there's nowhere left to run.

Amanda Leighton

I CANNOT WORD
(For my Lisa)

A stone unturned,
An envelope unopened,
A day has passed,
A memory has awoken.

Words of you have
Asked not to be spoken,
A knife in my heart,
A pain I cannot word.

My grief has no time,
Tears on my pillow
And as I lay you to rest,
A rose on your heart.
I will lay
Today, tomorrow,
Ten years from now,
Till the day I see you again.
All speak your name aloud,
My grief has no time.

Kirsty Keane

WOMEN

Women want to be blessed
Women want to be loved
Women want to be counted
Women want to be seen
Women want to be considered weak and able
Women want to be there
Women want to be in a good relationship
Good husband, lovely children, good home
Good times with friends, sisters, brothers

Women want not to be beaten by men
Women want not to be called hopeless
Women want not to be abused spiritually, physically, verbally,
Emotionally or psychologically
Women want to be free from violent men, workaholics and womanisers.
Women want to be free from worries.
Women want to be special
Women want to be respected and loved
Women don't want to be called names
Women want to hear, 'I love you'. 'You look nice'.
Women want to be huge in order
Women want to be appreciated, women really want to be loved.

Augustina Anane

COMPANIONS

Wearily,
I seek shade on the patio at noon.
Resentfully
Prepare my daily ration of pills
And eat breakfast.
The sun's glare shrivels my soul.

Silently,
A blackbird alights on a flagstone.
Delicately
Hops to a bowl of murky water
Left in a mellower moment
Then spreads his wings in salute.

I chew, he sips.
In the jungle of my pocket-size garden
A breeze caresses the leaves of the crab apple,
And rosebuds swell voluptuously in the sun,
As smiling,
I greet the day.

Valeria Brown

SUNDAY EBBING

Sunday ebbing
    like a tide sluicing time
polishing the jagged stones of last night
    smoothed, like a sky
settling, a gull on a crag
    and driftwood, leaving us little messages
        on this Sunday ebbing.

Trevor Landers

THE DATE

Preceded by a trumpet of Joy
she enters the room,
twisted hair adorned by her wedding hat,
moulting feathers trembling.
On sagging shoulders the mouldy fox
snuggles, its leering face in her chest.
Best dress droops as she sits
as regally as her bent spine will allow;
face alight with excitement,
mouth lopsided with stale crimson
she waves imperiously.
Let him in dear - don't keep him waiting.
Shining eyes fix on his face,
eating every word,
head bobbing to and fro
like a curious bird.
Flirtatious giggles - hand to mouth -
a teenager again.
Breathes - *Oh no - really - well I never.*
Then, too soon, it's over,
he says *Goodnight,*
her eyes fill with tears.
She stares at the space that was him.
I like to see him she whispers,
to hear his news, to catch up.
Her eyes filter bewilderment, fear, anger.
I hold my breath, choke on my love.
Time for bed then, love.
Recognition - resignation. Sadly,
Oh well, he'll be back tomorrow.
I turn off the television.
She takes my arm.

Dawn Voice-Cooper

WORKERS IN THE DARK

Delicate fingers stripping
Shards of raw wood
Is rain sounding on glass.
Touch, touch, touch. Nails
Long, pointed nails, pick,
Patiently strip. Go and come.

A distant groan as from the
Stomach of the old house
Is rumbling, growling.
A smart crack of the cat flap
Admits who, or whose
Scampering feet
Glad to reach home
Carrying rodents as prizes.

Twanging of pipe strings assaulted by
A violin learner, attempts by a cellist
To test out loose strings sharply
Seem tunelessly in tune, tuning-fork wise.
Exhausts, muffled by walls and
Double glazing, herald the odd nightly
Traveller. Workers in the dark.

Diane Burrow

WRITTEN IN THE RAIN

It's raining, prisons of diagonal slashing water
Smack the outside world.
Dark shapes huddle and slosh along teeming streets
I remain curled
In my chair, lost in the pages of a book
Where the sun always shines.
I plan my escape from the sodden soaking misery
To fairer foreign climes.
But, what is this, have the torrents abated?
Perhaps I'll stay.
Hot and distant places are such a bore
With sun every day.

Irene Brown

THE WIND HAS NEVER SHAKEN LEAVES SO GREEN

The wind has never shaken leaves so green,
Nor the sun shone sands so golden,
The snow has never fallen flakes so white,
Nor the stars twinkled skies so blue,
The lightning has never forked flashes so purple,
Nor the moonlit nights so black,
Since the rain has ceased to come
And the planets stopped their orbits.

Joe Loxton

FUTURE DREAMS

Waves splashin'
Bodies sinkin'
Hearts in turmoil
Bough breakin'
Minds irrationally thinkin'
Hold on, let go, love, hate, ice-cold
Talking, screamin' wishin'
If, but hope, no hope
Despair, dyin' cryin'
Can they cope
The ones that live
Survive the lives the dead give
Waves still splashin'
Titanic sinkin'
Minds forgotten, not thinkin'
Titanic forgotten, never, nor
The loved ones who died, their souls,
The unforgotten, the unforgiven
Or are they?

C Degan

THE ATTIC WALL

I was found behind a pile of dusters,
                         yellow old papers.
The smell of dust everywhere,
                         dirty well worn for that was me.
Soon dust was being brushed away from my papers.
                         And the papers being turned over one by one.
Soon my pages were being turned over and read very slowly,
                                        then tears filled his eyes,
for the lovely poems met his eyes.
                         For pride and love,
                                  he felt inside,
                                        for the pile,
                 of dusty old papers,
                                  top floor along the attic wall.

Iris Davey

THE OXFORD CIRCUS

The number thirty-seven goes there every day
but the one I'm going to talk about is a long way away.
There are bulls, snakes, lions and lizards
there are storms in tea cups, chill frosts and blizzards.
The snakes are beady-eyed, long and bald-headed
the fish drink like whales and need to be steadied.
The bulls are like twins, two peas in a pod,
they never agree but just smile brightly and nod.
The lion is tamed, the house cat is vicious
gossip is rife, untrue and malicious.
The lizard is obedient, his personality shredded
he thinks what the majority think lest he be beheaded.
The lion tamer is proud and continually cracks her whip
she speaks in soft tones, she's flamboyant and hip.
The stars of the show though are undeniably canine
their only cares in the world are 'when do we go walkies'
and 'what time do we dine?'
It's explosive and dangerous if you're not part of the troop
it can be heard from the galley, 'Let the peasants eat soup.'
It's absolutely fabulous, it's completely bizarre,
if you want to come in leave your tears in a jar.
Paint on a smile, be sure not to frown,
jump a few hoops and make like a clown.

Paula Daniels

GENEROUS TIMES OF PEACE

Never say never there's always time to get together
Encouraging words should be heard
Let's make peace, be good to all with ease
A kind gesture will not upset ya
Encouraging times a friendly drink is fine
A friendly smile gives comfort for a while
A walk in the park makes happiness an art
A gentle hug shows care and love
A loving kiss brings bliss
All the birds bring joy when heard
Bring pleasure to your loved ones forever
Time for goodwill, keeps minds so still
Be generous to the ones you know
Show peace to the ones who come and go.

Michael Norman Darvill

DEATH IN AUTUMN

Menace, such menace
in wrinkled brown leaves
heaped together
in a corner of the lift.

When the lift stopped,
between floors, the leaves,
stood on stalk ends and marched
towards the man in the centre.

The man, white faced,
isolated within six sides,
turned cold watching
the leaves reach his feet

then climb

up both his legs
over his stomach,
passed the chest and neck
until they reached his chin

where they paused,

only for a moment,
to enjoy the fear,
then advance slowly
to cover the head.

With a flutter he expired,
falling erect
through the open doors
of a now obedient lift.

Godfrey Dodds

THE DEIL AT WARK

The licht's gane oot an lourd's ma hert;
The warld's a cauldrife place.
Aathing's flat an colourless
an deid - an animated face!
The impact on the soul o man
is ane o total loss.
He's waa far doon in self esteem
hidden deep amang the dross
o ruined attitudes o mind
that bravely ta'en in righteous wrath
hae slowly dwined 'til noo they're but
the insubstantial froth
o ephemeral words in fleetin time
sae lichtly passed without a thocht
atween twa souls that cleave thegether,
resultin' in the damage wrocht.
The scars are left on ane an t'other
an come the nicht when aa's forgien
nae mair will ill-chosen words be tossed
t'ween t'wined herts or, a'm a mista'en?

Andrew A Duncan

MY NEW FOUND FRIEND

I found a new friend.
A short while ago,
Who picked me up
When I was low.
Who made me smile,
When I was down.
And when I was upset,
He played the clown.

With his warm gentle voice
He dried all my tears.
And we talked for hours,
Although seeming like years.
And he pulled me out
Of the hole I was in.
Broken out of my shell
And it's all thanks to him.

And now I grow stronger
Day after day.
And now is the time
That I feel I must say,
That you are the best
You made me feel new.
And I am so glad
To have a friend like you.

Helen Davis

WHEN I BECAME VOGUE

Out of my shell meet my kin.
Entered without choice but free of sin.
On the 15th Nov 1967.

By two I knew Santy, not yet Heaven.
By four I knew more, far too much by seven.
On the 15th of Nov 1974.

Two years in school, two years out the door.
Two years with friends, two years of war.
I yearn the 15th of some years before.

And now 'tis November 1984,
Long to get out and even the score.
Don't want the 15th anymore.

Forgot to remember to forget,
How once when young was let,
Savour the 15th of November any year.

Nov 2002 two marbles with tear.
The past crept up recall the fear.
'Return my 15th of Nov 1967!'
Or was that a second past Heaven.

Davide A Bermingham

THE MAD BARDS

('What do they think has happened, the old fools . . .'
Philip Larkin, 'The Old Fools')

What do they reckon on proving, the mad bards,
To be as mad as this? Do they maybe retard
Each adult, even gesture, that they might rule
The circumflex of wailing? Don't they recall
That madness is a matter that's enslaved?
Or is it more that they have been connived
On a mode of thinking which enclaves the law
Of thinking? Can it be that they really side
With the w*****s and the loners; that they rise
Each evening from their beds into a maw
Of blinking? If so (and it must be) it is mad!
    Why in hell's name are words perplexing?

In time, rhymes diminish: the words you've had
Start weedling away into rackish doom.
It is only oblivion that saves us from the flume
Of arid wordiness and all it gives.
The rhyme in youth is riled with moons; yes,
Mental corrosion takes its time to wind; but
The lack of knowing; the lack of regal tunes
Is all that makes the composed rhymester
Briar into contagion; so see it's so
That the brink of being mad is all that's left
Between the eager ranter and the flow
    Of rhymefulness into a mind bereft.

Perhaps being mad is having a lathe within
Turning and turning the mind into the dust
Of idle moving! Say then, that it is so
That the times we spend in meditation are
Just a proof of madness in the long-run.
Each mind has its own distinction and
In loitering annals, mental woes to stave;
But instinctively, the turning of a hand
Is final and enough to paint the grave
With instant ends: setting down a chair;
Moving through the lamp light, how despair
    Whisks the compos mentis through its trends

And into time; more, the endless regimens
Of hours and seconds, minutes, weeks and years
Is where the axis is at: this has to be
What deception and perception's all about:
The peaks and troughs, the highs and lows; the tears
Are here conceived into a rink of rhyme
That cuts the brain to pieces as it rears
And shaves away the spheres into quicklime!
These mad bards are not so foolish now -
Their distinct ways of seeming mad are fine!
See how their cranked and crazy lips sip wine
    And slip their eager girls the golden bough.

Jim Bellamy

JOE THE BUSKER

No more will Joe be seen
Strumming his old guitar,
While the passers-by make the scene
Look like a film shot from afar.
Every day he used to play
And sing songs of country style -
But he'll do it no more in any way
Cos he went that extra mile.
The man on the door of the store
Outside which Joe had his pitch
Was a brave security guard and more -
When it came to protecting that which
He believed in - fair deals, honest tasks,
A pleasant word as shoppers went in
And out of the store.
                    The baddies wore masks
As they robbed the store - rantin'
And ravin' they tried to run
But the man at the door said, 'No!'
And raised his fists to them until he was done
A mighty, wounding harm. It was Joe
That then stood in their ravishing way
Of escape - and he made them stop
Until others came running to take them away.
But Joe paid the price for being brave on top
Of being a mate of the man at the door.
They'd sore wounded John in his uniform black -
But they'd killed poor musical Joe before
His mate had time to pay him back
For defending the door of the store.

S V Batten

MANKIND

Heroes of the past and present
Rippling muscles everywhere
Personalities clashing
The selfishness of man causing wars
Man mating to produce the next generation
Man living life to the full
People trying to live in harmony
Working hard to make a living
Clashing with the colour of skin
A materialistic man turning money into his idol
Some devoting their lives to God
Living off the bounty of the land
The young are nurtured by their elders
Building structures to house himself
Using strength to construct many things
Showing the hand of friendship
Playing the sport of men
Filling their stomachs to the full
Giving balance between war and peace
May mankind survive on the face of this earth.

Joy Bartelt

RELATIVES

The mist cleared and the moon was
full and beautiful in his distant space.
The stars swarmed around and guarded
their father like all good children do.

Then one of them fell from the sky
and broke into a million pieces.
The moon cried silently as the sun
replaced him at dawn in his brightness.

He has no children to lose, only himself
in all his splendour to be concerned about.
His colder brother, the earth, circled him,
the weight of all his children on his back.

As they fought in some parts
they blasted holes into his ancient back.
As they travelled aimlessly in other parts
they wore his tired surface away.

And the tears of those who cried and prayed
for peace flowed like a river
while those who didn't care
tore out his heart with their evil laughter.

John Michael Doherty

HE IS MY BROTHER ALSO

The face is broad
Eyes echo my father
This lover warm, clean and solitary
Free to take his pathway
Is oblivious of my concern
Which in its selfishness
Seeks to bind and control

Unusual action
But he is kindred
There is recognition of self
In male form
Not found in previous bonding
Which when viewed thro'
Rose-tinted spectacles appeared unique
Eyes blinded by inexperience
And the wrong lenses.

Freedom then for this lover-brother-self
Still progressing
But still two steps behind.

Observing his elation
How could I not be happy?
He is my brother also.

June Drysdale

PREMONITION

Before I can even begin to take stock
My first memories of warmth and security
Are the sounds of the pushchair
Rumble bumping beneath me, little stones
Crinch crunching and the feeling
That I am in the tenderest, safest hands.
Kicking at mum from beneath the table
As she gets on with the dishes
While I give her peace and play
In the ever expanding world of imagination.
Then mum says, 'What tune keeps
Repeatedly going through my head?'
And I hazard a guess,
Progressing slowly but surely
Guided by astute, perceptive impulses. Anon
I remember staring out of the window -
Transfixed by the horror of
Something horribly wrong which might happen
As I tentatively watch her, almost in slow motion
Making her way through time and space
Across the road opposite our house.
While my dad makes a daft comment
To lighten up my solemnity.

Forty years later, she slipped
At that exact same spot where I had shown
Such irrational fear. She lay
For twenty minutes, under a tree
Pinioned with pain which I found
Incomprehensible. Dad phoned
And I was there instantly
With him joking 'Pain?
You don't know what pain is!'

I held her hand in the ambulance
As she groaned involuntarily
At every bump over uneven ground.
Dad's face went beetroot when he recognised
Her femur had been broken.
My ultimate fear had been realised.

Yet with her usual, remarkable resilience,
Mum hoisted herself up the bed,
Commented on how unexpected her new
Situation was and cheerfully chirped
That she'd just have to adjust to it
The way she'd told us
To accept the inevitable.
With that insuperable
Coping mechanism in full swing
All I could do was marvel
That my premonition
Had not heralded
The end but the beginning
Of another learning experience
From life's worthy transcender.

Dianne Aspey

A DUE 60S DIRECTION

Our local park ran aground on
Reefs as pointed as the reasons why
Kids wash up on needles. When the
Wind blows from a due 60s direction,
It's cold where once it was so warm.
Climate change I suppose. But this wind
Kind of took the park unawares when
Becalmed with bird aviary and tennis courts.
It had a rudder made of families staying together
And a deck for old folk, with band stand
And bowling green Sundays spent putting gossip.

What appears to have happened
Is this wind sprang up and glass bottle shard
Pavilion window memories of my childhood,
Splattering graffiti like cider all over them.
The toilets became the open sex sort,
The wind breaking down barriers
Of decorum and taboo -
Sweeping from the park's once steady platform
Ghosts of many cowboy games
And evening walks on parent hand
By flower beds smelling of cultivated Vimto.

The park, driven now,
Stove up on a board announcing:
Keep off. Closed until further notice.
At a point where there's
Rock after rock of those needles,
Together with youths
Playing games
I daren't but understand
And might have joined in with
Were I younger
As I also blew in from a due 60s direction.

Peter Asher

WHY ME?

Why is it always me,
That has to change plans constantly?
Fitting in with other people's ideas,
They are all smiles,
I am close to tears.
But, they don't seem to care,
I think it is so unfair,
But I have a secret plan, that they
Don't know,
I am making plans to go.

After all, I have a life of my own,
But they won't leave me alone,
Messing around with my plans and dreams,
I don't count, or so it seems,
But when I am not around, just you wait,
Maybe then they will appreciate,
The favours I did them by the score
And they will miss me not being there anymore.

Maureen Arnold

WEATHER TO BE OR NOT TO BE

Some people appear to be shut in the dark
With nothing to look forward to
With gales and storms and haze all around
Stay indoors what else can they do?

With frost and cold to chill their bones
With no hope in the future to come
Hurricane, cyclone and squall are ahead
Misery and torment can't be fun.

Now others most definitely have found the light
With everything going for them
Enriched in the sun to warm their hearts
Spreading The Gospel to women and men.

The light breezes they comfort and help them along
The pathway of brightness and ecstasy
Friendly dedication to succeed in their faith
That's how it is for me.

C Armstrong

THE SEAGULLS' CRY

I hear the seagulls' cry

As I look above me
The rolling hills behind me seem in some way out of place,
or is it me?

As the sun beats down onto the concrete slabs,
it glares from the windows into my tired, weary eyes,
as I sit quietly.

People around me, rushing from one place to another,
like there isn't enough time left - for what?
I don't know.

Suddenly a busker starts playing in the background
Dulling the noise of traffic with a tune, vaguely familiar,
but I'm not quite sure.

Lovers walk by, hand in hand,
staring into each others eyes, nothing else matters.
A cyclist pushes past, destroying their fairy tale.

Rain starts falling,
forcing people to retreat to the dryness of the shops.
It's quieter now, only the faint murmur remains.

The busker stops playing,
as the sun reveals the mountains once more,
that are far beyond the town.

I hear the seagulls cry.

Amy Zeglicki

THE WATCHER

She watches me, the watcher,
No words does she impart,
Still, I can tell just from those eyes
The love stored in her heart.
I've seen inside her very soul,
And held it in my grasp,
But the watcher just keeps watching
Till I've had my repast
And then her eyes lock onto mine,
I'm captivated once again,
She takes me to her dreamland,
I'm on some heavenly plain.
Don't ever stop watching me,
Lock me up in your heart,
Throw away the key,
The watcher will always be watching,
The watcher will always have me!

M B McLaughlin

BEYOND WISHES

If my heart should stop
And my body be carried into a sea of darkness
Carry me on
And if this breath should be my last
May my soul stay with yours
And unite as one
For God need never divide us
We are two halves of one whole
My heart may not beat or have use anymore
But will remain with you and your soul.

Wendy Jane Langton

RAROTONGA 2

A big, fat cockroach
    Sitting in my mealmates
        Friendly gecko just slithered across
            the slanting wall
Cook Island melody resounding
in the distance
    Coconut oil scent in the air.
        My body twitching
        Pulsating through the endless heat
            of the night.

Christina C Simpson

RAIN

As I got up this morning
And looked out my windowpane
I couldn't believe it
It was pouring down with rain

The day it poured with rain
Is a day I will never forget
It really put me in a bad mood
And I also got soaking wet

Working in the rain
Can give you such a cough
It really could have waited
Till I can have my day off

I only like sunny days
To me, they are a must
Because I don't want to end up
Just another heap of rust

David Sheasby

Two Hundred Miles To Greenwich

Out from the confines of Wallingford
Past the old churches at Oxford
Down a path by the Thames
Through centuries of people in chains
To Hackney carriages of old
Past gibbets and houses dearly sold
The silver threads of water
That doesn't really alter
As pleasure boats wait at the lock
And swans gracefully flock
Jets pass loudly overhead
Past another mock Tudor in Hampstead
Into the city and past Putney Bridge
Away from the rusty fridge
Standing out in glue like mud
As a barge passes with a thud
The sun glints off the Bloody Tower
As ravens watch and glower
History oozes from river pores
As civil servants play with new laws
Trees overshadow the foot path
Braving the weather's wrath
Footsteps still pad along a tow path
Night flows like a whistler painting
The air over the river isn't for tainting.

Tim Sharman

BIG KIDS

Kids with bigger bodies, bigger heads and bigger hands,
Making all those gestures at me, making plans and demands.
They're making love, we're making do,
They're making me, they're making you.
Making noise, making ploys,
Making employees into toys.
Bleak to weak and weak to bleak,
Five out o' seven in this coming week.
Nine to five, nine to nine in time,
Making war not in their hours, but in yours and mine.
Kids with bigger bodies overtake in fast cars,
But legs not as strong as ours!
I'm telling what I know, but they make truth, they make lies,
Now it's at our kids that they're making eyes.
Got to take a breath now, this death is getting to me . . .
(Of course, if I die sure they'll make haste to dig me up and sue me.)
And charge me with feeling, believing what's mine,
All because I did it in work time.

Dave Skelton

ANGELOLOGY

Lady from America -
Where all things happen now -
Has found the way to open routes
Of discourse with the angel-kind
Who tenuously, it would seem,
Inhabit regions in-between
The worlds we see and do not see,
Intermittently - has found a way
Of making clear connections with
Their hovering selves and us;
And strengthening their ties with us
To our great benefit. All of which
She will communicate to us
For simple fees in daily schools
Of twenty pounds per session -
With some refreshment extra.
Never fear, she has degrees to prove her worth -
The highest that America provides -
So take advantage:
Bind some angel to your service.

Joe Smedley

MY DIET

I really have been naughty
Again I have eaten too much
My tummy feels like a balloon
And my bra's ready to burst
I keep saying I must slim
Get my figure neat
But every minute that I sit
I feed my face in sweets
Sometimes it is chocolate, cakes or biscuits
Ice cream, hard sweets or popcorn
Then I tell myself I will eat tonight
And start my diet in the morning
Morning comes to my diet I stick
I'm being a really good girl
But by 6.00pm I'm at it again
And my diet's gone over the hill
I really must try to cut out all sweets
And I know I will do it this time
I will be good, all day on my diet I'll stay
And I won't eat any sweets until nine.

M E Smith

LONG PAST BEDTIME

I must stay awake, but Sleep is on the warpath,
Pressing behind my eyes, getting abusive -
'Hey you, you unmade bed!
Make yourself! Tidy yourself! Give me stretching room!'

I try reasoning -
'You know how it is, Sleep.
One of these frantic days, deadlines crowding.'

'Crowd them somewhere else, not strewn all over my bed!
Such shoddy service!'

I try assertion -
'Now look here, sleep was made for people, people weren't made
                                                    for sleep.
I'll sleep when I'm - hey, go easy on my eyes!
If once they close -'
They do.
Sleep heaves the clutter off his bed.
His snores drown out this silly poem.

Joe Solomon

THE ROCK SO BIG, EVEN GOD CAN'T MOVE IT

Terminal illness. Cancer.
An object immovable in this universe.
I push up my sleeves, to lend my strength,
Put my shoulder to this big rock regardless . . .
And can't budge it a goddamn inch.

But then what was I expecting?
To reach in, through his taut skin
and curl my fingers around the rigid black rock?
Yank it out hard and throw it far away?
Did I really honestly think that
I could cure that guy with my tenderness?

I'm ashamed to admit it, but yes.

The worst phrase in the world,
'There's nothing you can do'.
The door closes on the world,
We sink into cold darkness.

Leonie Smith

INNER TORMENT

This sea of conflict froths and harries
pounding jagged pebbles in my soul . . .
It strives to turn each one to sand
and clog the channels of emotion in flowing silt.
It strives in vain.
There is no time to smooth the tattered rocks.
Would that the tide forever turn, recede and leave the stones in peace -
thoughtless and unmoved.

W Ballantyne Scott

UNTITLED

As I stare
A beautiful bride smiles back
Golden blonde hair with
Red flowers
Reflecting her strong personality
That was what he liked about her
Eyes so blue and clear
And full of fun
He will like her choice
Silky white dress falls
Over her slim petite body
Diamonds sit neatly
Around her neck and
Down the length of her gown
As she takes one last look
Dad takes her hand and
Seals it with a kiss

Rachel Baldwin

THE DREAMER

His eyes glassy sea, of Ultramarine
    that only yesterday knew pleasure.
Relaxed now; to blank expression,
    lack of memory, transfixed his face.

Crossing over was easy
    freed from bodies suffering.
A watermark, translucent, serene
    Indelibly written in the hearts, of friends.

A single thread windblown, in air
    memories fragile substance.
A blur of flowers and sympathy
    in the sweet smell, of new mown grass.

Cold brass, glinting in brilliant sun
    warming the old bones, of carved oak.
The dreamer drifting in time, unaware
    dreamed; silently on.

Had no knowledge of pale faces, like chalk
    tear stained and sober; in their grief.
And the black shadows they cast
    huddled together, words in hushed whispers.

The stillness of a library on a Monday
    polite enquiries, inconsequential, small talk.
More words from the bible, music
    and then, eternity.

Jane Bagnall

CREDIT CARD BLUES

I'm up to my neck in debt
Now they won't let me forget
I've got letters from creditors
Stuffed in a drawer
I'm worried because it's never happened before
My bedroom's packed out with clothing and shoes
Nobody knows why I'm suffering the blues
The first time I used my credit card
I found it so easy, I just couldn't stop
Well you know the old saying
Shop till you drop
Where will I get the money from
To pay for all the things I can't wear?
Maybe I should change my name and address
Then, I wouldn't have a care.

James Ayrey

WORLD CUP FOOTBALL - ENGLAND V COLUMBIA 1998

Transmitted soccer to The Crispin
in name of shoemaker saint
Victory on his day was Agincourt
'God for Harry England and St George'
as Shakespeare wrote in 'Henry V'
Boots are on to take world name
Global challenge to England's game
played in the days of Henry.

Cross of St George to football
red; on background white
marking the Crusades
now T-shirts, bath towels, painted hands
decorated faces for battle
'banner hung' from bedroom windows
worn as capes by boys
convoy size on cars and lorries.

Union flag in second place
Welsh and Scottish devolution
Red and upright cross alone
supported by the churches
England's Agincourt identity
though Henry used Welsh archers
and flags of George and Andrew
reconcile on public houses.

The games afoot to cheering
will St Crispin hold the sway?
A goal! An English goal!
thunders through the terrace houses
- but now the wounded grooms
and dreadful words at TV set
Outside voices - consolation
'They don't deserve - it should be ours.'

Crusader inspiration wanes
to loss of football popularity
- and with each banner folded
how might the next reaction be
for April 23rd: St George's Day
with red cross flying high
shall the old supporter say
'There's no world football on?'

Reg C H Baggs

ARGUMENT

Broken arrows, twisted words
Mar the paper of our sovereignty.
The canvas of the mind
Just within our reach
Though no grip can control.

How many words can make a truth
Or speeches truth a lie?
So intent to see beyond
This poor reflection
And clean the dark and frosted window.

Emma Ayling

A Job

Busy people.
Rushing here, rushing there.
Lucky people.
Things to do, jobs to go to.
Learn they said.
Study hard they said.
Get a good job they said.
But they didn't say where.
Sorry they said.
No vacancies they said.
No jobs they said.
Better luck next time they said.

Jo Hannon

WATCHING

She looked through the window
As people passed by
At normal folk with normal lives
And all she could do was cry

Thinking of a time when she was so carefree
Could go where she wanted to
Free as a bird in flight
Lived every day as normal folk do

But now she's in torment
Struggling to get out of the door
She's on the edge and fearful
Her nerves are jagged and raw

So a lonely figure she stands
Her lot in life to be endured
By the window wistfully watching
Praying one day to be cured

Lynda Long

EXQUISITENESS

The depth of my misery was
So great, so great!
All my anguish, heartache, heartache.
When upon my pillow
The tears they fell,
They fell.
Then gave I away my burden.
I carried a new and lighter load.
A weight that was weightless.
I forgave.
Now my spirit is so great,
So great!
See.
I hurt no more,
No more.
Do thou likewise and
Be blest.

Ronald D Lush

RIDING ON A NIGHT

How harsh storms rip and rage the sky
In darkest hours after sweet lullaby
To bring us light when hides the moon
Near frantic rocks where once it loomed.
You count the seconds from strike to flash
And wonder if its eye has passed.
Through fervent night and frosty air
The threat of rain lies everywhere.
Those evening birds that fly low and wild
Wail feverously like sulking child.
Light a fuse, the panic deep
Why such nightmares taint your sleep.
Yet here is safety, here is peace
To where can birds and bats retreat?
The call is high and the hour low
Crash! One, two, three, and then the glow.
It rides above, the pressure's high
As the air of Heaven and Hell collide.
Heart strikes 4, 5, 6 - the pain!
From why silent skies comes such rain?
When early sun broke through morning mist,
Onto our skin her warmth she kissed.
Though now beneath the oceans great
She waits alone for dawn to break.
And whilst we toss in broken slumber
Winds lift the clouds, displacing thunder
Its journey carries to islands new
But has left its trace of fear in you.

Laura Lang

RADIO SILENCE

My radio has been turned the way of nations,
lost in soul and lost in patience;
It leaves me with a soundless morning,
heavy as clay upon the lighted room,
filling its voids with despair and gloom.

Just a thought, just a notion,
skimming birds across an ocean.
Snowdrops blowing in the wind,
virginal white with deep devotion.

Keep their date from year to year,
hang their heads if to shed a tear.
Their ephemeral visit so short in time,
leaves this poet with only rhymes . . .
and radio silence.

Thomas Allan Liddle

COMMUNITY

Community, a feeling almost sacred in our family;
following our marriage we were perturbed
we could not beget children;
my wife, time and again, treated in hospital,
medical advice, just keep trying,
never occurring to the medicos to check on me!
It still does not prevail to them -
assuming all males are born perfect!

I discovered about myself during a medical,
necessary obligation in taking an endowment policy,
'You have two children I note,' said the MO,
'adopted I presume, as you have only one testicle.'
Our family community co-joining continually,
the children - boy and girl - growing in their years,
we slipped into a joint proprietorship
without impairment of individual rights.

We, children and parents, so closely bonded together -
something so other-worldly than genetics -
now, close community leading into wider community,
great occasion of our daughter's wedding!
Arrival of grandchildren.
Our son not yet attaining this other closeness.
Now, in our advanced old age - departure apprehending
to a possible new community unending?

Jim Lucas

SPRING MEMORY

Down a green damp lane
Where twigs crackle beneath my feet,
Searching for soft primroses
Hidden near lichened fallen trees
I saw last autumn's bracken
And found a path which came
To meet me like a friend.
The silvered bark lay mossy, torn
In crumbled shards. I trod green fronds
Of newborn growth,
Saw a grey stone wall
And found a church, ivied and worn
By gentle time. Even now
High tangled hedges undisturbed
Unbroken, embrace those graves,
With worn and loving words
Engraved there in a time long passed,
And never seen, nor wept over, nor spoken.
A blackbird on a bough
Spiked with white blossom sprang his song
With joy, wet violets
Curled in woody tangy scent
Guarded the church, had veined
Their leaves against those walls so long
As if in charmed protection.
I found that path, and wandered there,
And still I smell the spring-warmed scents
Of dampened leaves and soft brown earth,
That bittersweet remembered joy
Within my dreams - upon their air.

Janet Morgan

THE TRENCH

There was the smell of
Gunpowder in the air
That cold November night.
The shell shot troops,
Huddled up in their
Bunkers, within the
Ten foot trench.
The trench was wet and
Damp, those men were icy wrecks,
Frozen by the cold and fear
Of the hell above, and
The rain kept pouring down.
Those trenches were the tombs
Of many a good man, their
Life long desire, wiped out.
In ten seconds of sheer
Madness blitzed by bombs
And bullets flying wildly about.

R Murray

THE STRANGER

There she is again,
Looking in my window.
Her face has no expression for me to read
Standing motionless, she gazes in,
I return her stare,
Daring not to blink,
For if I do
I'll find she is not there.

I wonder why she comes,
What it is she could want
Is it me she comes to see?
Or is there another image,
Out of my view?
I'd turn and look,
But if I do
I'll find she is not there.

Annette Murphy

A NEW WORLD

It dragged, dirty,
In wonder-works and mirror-ponds:
Unusual though
In its prickly steel
And dancing wings.
The order of the day
Matched to winnowing surf -
The stretched line
Of the golden horizon.
It works at midday mostly
Crabbed in hollows of angelica
And oriental spice.

It is the burning of the violet flame
For forgotten memories.
It is too soon and too late now for thought:
The patchwork of seances
Hidden in our fragile mind's eye,
Holding seas of experience
In the twinkle of Russian nights
And daisy chains.
We are older now
Handing down our wisdom
To the next generation.

It is changing again.
Imagine the Heaven beyond
The rolled up sky
Broken only by sideways clouds
Dipped in alizarin textures,
Born again each second
In liquid form.

For we are in our element
Under cloaks of rainbows.
It may be we are what we are -
Nearer to earth and stone
Blown to ashes
On a fading wind
Both peasant and king.

Live life now, deeply,
And never regret
Things done and undone.
The sharp cry hits again
And the mind
Gently settles
On a new world.

Peter Corbett

IT HAPPENS

Fallen for a charmer? Once in a while
you want to soak it up - the potent blue
eyes, the easy grace, the wonderful smile.

It's usually when life seems to pile
on the crap that, weakened, you crave things true
and easy: *please, just this once in a while*

let things be simple, let there be no guile
in the world, or calculation. So you
let yourself be charmed - blue eyes, gentle smile -

and then lose yourself in fantasy (hell,
it's better mapped than life), wildly dreaming you
can charm this charming prince but all the while

knowing, too, you should be running a mile
from such prodigal beauty. Join the queue
for the blue-eyed, charming, wonderful smile.

And so, tears before bedtime. Denial
of touch and love does cruel things to you.
We've all been there. Every once in a while
blue eyes charm you from your wondering smile.

Lucy Crispin

BEAUTY

Rain is beating on my windowpane,
The cold wind howling outside,
I take pleasure in some flowers,
A warm glow I feel inside.

These flowers are called carnations,
All typed with the same name,
Yet, as I look more closely,
No two are exactly the same.

Each one an individual,
A shape and style their own,
Beauty from them radiates,
Their blossom now fully grown.

The colour of a fire's ember,
A beautiful deep amber glow,
Yet if you observe them completely,
Their hues are different you know.

My thoughts go a stage further,
As the truth I now incur,
The tears in my eyes are swelling,
Physical vision now a blur.

For with the recognition of beauty,
Comes humbleness you see,
For these flowers are God's creation,
Without God, nothing could ever be.

So as I put this point to you,
In this way I try to explain,
Did the carpenter make the wood,
Or smooth it with his plane?

Christine Cyster

Dreams By The 'Pond Of Horus'

To flood the Shihor river with a row of kites pulling boats
riding on water ponies, little waves woolly wild.
Falcons smile down, one-eyed profiles from masted flags, bronze boys
hold steady the ropes, ready to tag or firl the cloth
in a sort of quaint flamingo dance, Egyptian style.

A warm wind smells of river water, rushes big as bulls.
A plaintive spiralling bird cries, torn through empty skies
in aimless-seeming eddies, calling, calling.

D Burrow

UNTROUBLED MIND

At night, review wise thoughts of yesteryear.
The woe that seems so new to you is old.
In other places, other times, the strain
Of trouble made the thoughtful pen response.

For instance: 'work the best narcotic is';
And 'don't despair, but if you do, work on';
Plus 'act for good and hope for good and take
What comes' - all formulas for fortitude!

'This day,' Columbus wrote determinedly,
'We sailed on,' adding just, 'course west, south west.'
What difficulties did this brief note shield?
'We cry inside,' a recent version says.

Such lines-to-live-by force our hopes to rise.
'Make me an instrument of peace,' we cry,
And reap the calm from heartfelt hide-and-seek,
Recov'ring thought and feeling lost just now.

All wisdom to the same conclusion comes.
For one thing only any price is worth.
'On my head, pour a sweet serenity.
Untroubled mind, please give me now,' I pray.

Allan Bula

TRANSFIXED

Loves temple lures me in
incense heady like lover's wine
hypnotic neath the starry face of night
Whereupon you bare your nakedness
transfixed, your body nestles up to mine
and sets two hearts alight

On fragrant soft pillows His and Hers
you lie, untamed and curious
reclining on designer's linen
your fingertips tracing buds and blossom.
Let me lead you in this lovemaking,
let our wild hearts pulsate in time
and your feelings run through mine

Let me lead you in this love of ours
sighing, weeping in wild ecstasy
allow yourself to be a part of me.
Let me lie elated midst your thighs
passionately melt and flow
feel the fire, feel the glow
Slowly kiss and lose yourself in paradise

A million roses scent your dreams
transfixed your body nestles up to mine
on fragrant soft pillows His and Hers
you lie there, tamed in sheer bliss
Your fingertips tracing my lips

Beth Izatt Anderson

NIGHT RAIN

Unseen,
A greater darkness gathers in the night.
It is the Night-Rain Monk -
He spreads his robe across the sky.

The stars are extinguished,
And fall upon my roof-tiles.
'Tck, tck, tck',
Like Shiva's drum.

Droplets hang like pearls from the gutters.
A billion crystal worlds,
Each suspended in a linear cosmos.
They gather,
They swell -
And they are gone.

From a place of stillness,
On the very edge of dream,
I lie listening to the rain.
I am unperturbed -
I neither desire the storm,
Nor fear it.

I have sympathy,
For those who are caught in the downpour.

Philippa Adburgham

LAMENTATIONS
(The lovesick poet tells of his love)

Slow death that kills not I
But some whose wish is not so
When, I pray, will mine draw nigh
I love to love, yet to love I hate
For love like death, kills
Does the Devil ever fall in love?
Yet Hell's arms be warmer than a lover's despise
Love is no lady but a whore
Who despises this willing soul
For this flower too, once was gay
But a wondrous wind blew and all was still
How does it feel to love?
Is not to die, better still
For as long as the Devil wears no rosary
Bound I would be to my lover's will
And all will be hope and hope still

Anthony T Chirape

THIS PLACE

Between the hospital and the home
Runs a street
My street
It brought me here
Showed herself to me
Told me what I needed to know
Guided me through the dangers
And the places to avoid
Helped me to the warm places.
The doors educated
And the open market tested and shaped me
This street built me
I didn't ask it to
But it wrapped me in its arms
Approved my goal
And when I was ready
Kissed my brow
In farewell.

On the horizon is a map
Of this place
My place
It gave me identity
And chartered my course
When I asked for it
And then when I needed it
It added a past
To my present
Was patient with me
And when I was ready
Blessed my plan.

This place loved me
For what I am
Not as judge or juror
Did she comment
Just opened my door
And left it there

So this land
Which gave birth
To my place
And my street
Sits and waits
She doesn't demand
There is no need
A mother's way
is to cut the cord
Sooner, than later
A sacrifice of life
And what replaces the cord
Depends on both ends
To imagine it still there
Breathing for you
For this land
This place
This street

In this bag is a light
And I am the torch
But the bulb
Is here, with you
You are the fire
That made me warm
You illuminate my way
And I am drawn to you
Without need of sight
And with me I bring
All that I have found
To share with you

There are jewels here
In my pockets
And I was only allowed
To put them there
Because you gave me
The hands

Robert Chiswick

WHITE DOVE

Why has this world turned in to a heartless place?
Where people are discriminated, for their colour creed or race.
The wars are tearing families apart,
You sometimes think, do these purgatrators, really have any hearts?
Their lives are so full of destruction and grief,
In these war-torn countries, are the innocent ever going to
get some relief.
From the pain and suffering caused by these men.
Is all this pain and suffering really ever going to end?
We here are all close to *spirit* in our walks of life,
Our spirit guides walk with us all hand in hand,
They help change our ways and get us to understand.
We all here pray, every day every week,
To send healing thoughts, to the sick and the meek.
Let's pray and hope our words are all heard.
To these war-torn countries all over the world,
Where the fighting and anger rage through these lands.
Let's pray our good thoughts will help them understand.
There is not always hatred, there is harmony and love.
We all pray that they'll understand, the true meaning of *white dove . . .*

Diane Ennis-Chopping & Leau Chie

NEVER LEAVE ME LONELY

Never leave me lonely
never leave me blue
be my one and only
all life through
each new day we will
savour all love's joy anew, so,
Never leave me lonely
Never leave me blue

David A Bray

PARADISE LOST (FOREVER)

I can see a rainbow majestic in my mind,
So perfectly shaded even though I am blind,
Once able to see material entities,
I can now only imagine love - a love that I can seize.

Cast away on a merchant ship,
Fate believed it to be my final voyage - death it did equip
Though tossed into the water,
Waves of terror crashed into my weak body,
But I swam to shore with hope and glee.

Thinking I was the best,
Believing myself to be better than a
Peaceful feeling of acquiesce;
I stopped to rest upon an Island so pure,
But my conscience forced me to explore
The wonder - mine to endure . . .

Palm leaves brushed my rosy face
As I ascended a hill of grass-filled grace,
Oh, the view of golden sand,
Crashing waves unto the unspoiled land,
Exotic birds free from human hand
- Or indeed from any gun,
But I looked directly at the luring sun!
At all the rays that had been shone!
My eyesight hazy - but alas my eyesight gone!

Running (as if I had no time) through the Island I believed to be mine,
Frantically, for any form of help
No matter what the cost
Rescued from the Island of glorious vision,
My eyesight along with paradise was to be . . .
Forever lost.

Tim Coles

SPEAK TO ME OF LOVE

Write to me of love
Tell me what you feel
Speak to me of love that lasts
For our eternity.

Write to me of love
The love that knows no end
Meet me in that place
Where only lovers know.

Oh, tell me that such love exists
And tell me that I'll find it
Tell me that it can be found
On Earth as well as Heaven.

Or is all earthly love just fleeting
As we ourselves must be
Oh speak through all the strife and turmoil
Speak to me of love.

Opal Innsbruk

IT'S TRUE, I WAS THERE

A lot of noise came from an Angling Club, eating and drinking
At the rear of the pub, the landlord had me tucked in the Ingle
With a quiet man, enjoying his beer.
Laughing and bragging, and telling a few lies, telling of success
With their home-made flies, chap next to me said, 'I'm sorry
You must be bored, we enjoy our fishing, we get carried away.'
From his seat in the Ingle, fellow I sat with said, 'I was interested,
I would like to join in,' in a silence that could be cut with a knife.
Fishing last week, with a friend, he said a stretch we keep quiet.
Need a good boat, and a strong rod, a reel like a winch, big hook
Well dressed for salmon, with a very strong line. A big gaff
And rubber boots, much oversized, no socks, just a cap, a hat
It's deep out there, have to take care, I was soon into a big fish
We've had a few, but this was a biggy, took our boat where it wished
My mate had hold of me, teased him in, very slow
The nose came up, that mouth was enormous.
Mate yelled, 'Let him go,'
But I wanted him, and out he came, right over the boat,
The line caught everywhere, the rod got wedged, and we went in,
We grabbed the boat side and off with the clothes, I went under
My knife in its leather in my belt, eased out,
The fish was close, I grabbed a bit of that so-slippery fish,
And struck hard, it sunk out of sight, I had cut my line.
We lost a lot of tackle so what!
The fisherman had never moved, the others sat still, 'twas quiet.
The spokesman said after that, 'There is nothing I can say,
Your tale is the best I've heard today,
I trust such a fish never comes my way.'

H Cotterill

HEARTLESS WIND

Oh wicked wind, you stole my heart!
Through sanctuary you crept,
In dreams I saw you capture it,
As in 'Morpheus'' arms I slept.

The Earth's now home and I must roam:
Sweep plain, brush nook and crevice,
Toss quilts of corn where I was born -
To where my hidden heart is?
Blast wailing pots, gouge keyhole slots,
Skirt gaps in frames and trellis,
To mount the breeze, kiss quivering trees -
Well hid my wayward heart is!
I'll stalk the trail of Father Gale,
Your brother, Storm, must learn:
To Heaven above I've pledged my love,
So speed that dove's return!

Now - stolen heart can tear apart,
Please pity my dilemma,
There's one in wait, his claim to make
But will he wait forever?

Brenda Mentha

THE BABY DOLL

I went into the loft
Where it was cold and grey.
I went in search of yesterday.
I'd laid you gently in a box,
I couldn't part with you, you see.
Too big for dolls and yet
I wanted you to stay with me.

Red felt-tipped mouth, blue eyes that closed,
Black lashes, soft upon your cheek,
Brown pottery hair, so cold to touch
I loved you far too much.
Your body so soft and white,
Little brown arms outstretched,
Small red-tipped hands just wanting *me*
Parent and child, we bonded instantly.

At last I found you buried in the dark.
Yes! That's the box,
A brown old box, now turned to grey,
I couldn't part with you but why I cannot say.
I tore away the years
Amid a shower of dust and . . . sudden fears.
An old pot head looked out at me
From the one eye still in place,
An ugly rash of crumbling paint
Had disfigured part of your lovely face.

I washed your clothes, I washed your face,
Your brown pot legs that never stayed in place.
The closed eye opened and we stared,
Two strangers now today
For there's no way back to yesterday.

Pat Morton

RENEWABLE ART SOURCES

Wistful ambient music
fulfils the gallery.
Art nods, everso, at science
offering up new works.

A light sculpture,
previously unrendable,
sings in binary code
like wineglass tinkerings.

Rare plastic mouldings;
impossible configurations
shaped in zero gravity
affordable for very few.

Lifeforms of captured still-life.
Suspended animation
in a broth of space-age chemicals
never before available.

Audio-visual canvasses
recombining endless combinations
of computer generated
remote-controlled variation.

Triptych of electricity.
A molecular sketch.
Holographic portraiture.
Perpetual 3D visions.

A virtual exhibition place,
exclusively on-line.
Another installation sold
close to the speed of light.

Bruce McRae

TELE-VISION?

A flying spot by millions seen
Who gaze intently at the screen
Yet see no spot.

They see the spot blurred to a form
Which captures hungry minds forlorn
By life around.

Minds and bodies sapped all day
By men at work or children's play
Seek their escape.

The beauty of the world around
They do not see. Just underground
And office blocks.

No stimulation from without
Is like a long relentless drought:
There is no life.

In creative death they sit and stare
In silence from their own armchair
At other lives

Created by the vital few
Who try to show the tired sad view
Of how we live.

Some may see their message plain
But others seek to entertain
Themselves, not think.

The wondrous detail of this world
Alas to some is not unfurled;
No time to see.

And so they blunder blindly on
Until their span of years is gone
And it's too late.

The spot gives detail to the screen,
How sad that in life's broader scene
Some see no spot.

Douglas Bryan Kennett

SHADOW THEATRE

Outside, a parade of shadow puppets
line up and move at varying paces.
One leans over two sticks,
has an arched back and a rain hood.
I am back in the times of the Brothers Grimm:
that is the old Grandmother or the wolf
moving slowly in silhouette.

Then the nimble figure of a man
dances from right to left across the stage
which is the pavement outside my window.
He turns midway, gesturing against the air
as if to frighten off some invisible foe.
Perhaps it is the wind.

A hum and a brum
and a ladder fixed to a van moved on,
and one senses the hand of the puppeteer.
And then, for a moment or two
the stage is clear,
just light filtering through the panel
and distant rumblings of car engines
and hushings of tyres on tarmac,
and as night falls, the curtain comes down,
a nocturne in grey and blue,
and the shuffling of people going home.

Linda Landers

PAUSE AWHILE

Just pause awhile with me and look at all
the wonderful things -
That do not cost a penny -
A sweet scented rose,
wet with the early morning dew.
The intricate web a spider weaves,
frail delicate and new.
A blackbird, beady eyes, so cheeky,
Bathing in the small stone bath.
The squirrels, their antics in the trees,
really make me laugh.
Buttercups and bluebells
as I walk through the wood
The little signs of springtime,
When wild flowers come into bud
Waterfalls, like silver,
Gushing to the valley, far below.
Children, laughing, screaming as
they toboggan down the slopes,
In winter's crisp white snow.
All these things I love to see,
They always make me smile
So do not hurry by -
Just pause awhile.

Dorothy Chadwick

DELUSION

I boarded the valiant galleon, as it faced
the raging storm, and the rain lashed down,
and my hair danced out.
It stung my face, it made me shout,
As the thunder rolled and lightning flashed
(And I laughed out loud, at the scurrying crowd).

The sky grew black and dangerous,
Lightning shone, like a laser display
But I hung on fast, this could be the last
I heard a spoil-sport say!
(And I laughed out loud, at the scurrying crowd).

My clothes drenched, I couldn't see,
The force of the rain, was blinding me,
My heart beat faster, the storm grew darker,
I heard them shout 'You'll have to get out!'
(And I laughed out loud, at the scurrying crowd).

Wish I could have ridden that storm till it faded
and died, but they put up a sign . . . *Closed . . . Due
To Bad Weather!* Nothing more than a theme park ride!
(And I laughed out loud, as I joined the crowd . . .

Rose Childs

THE SACRED WORLD OF PISCES

To the sacred world of Pisces
The fostered disciples are drawn
And the heartbeat of Jerusalem
Will be host to their every dawn
Mercury rules these surrogate minds
Neptune sits on their platinum throne
The spirits of the Tigris and Euphrates
Will guard their spiritual home
Their soul is of Mediterranean beauty
Living in the colour of peace
And prayer is the holistic refuge
Where they store their religious belief
Rose coloured thoughts are resident
Bearing vague but ambitious schemes
And the world of hypochondria
Reach out into turbid dreams
Upon a promised imaginative horizon
The moonstone does emanate trust
Where sea-green auras are prominent
And the willow does bathe in musk
'Tis a colony of sensitive compassion
Marinating in easy going moods
On a mission to master reality
Where dreams and fantasies protrude
Sometimes lost in deserts of time
Sometimes lost in nebulous thought
But intuitive reason shines its light
Where truth has a constant rapport
They the embroiderers of beauty shall always be as one
In the eternal poem of Pisces that was written in Babylon

David Bridgewater

EVERY WRONG TURN

There will be a time for tears.
This isn't one.
Wait until the worst comes to the worst
and I see my daughter
in the arms of another man.
Then I'll let my feelings out.

I know the kind of guy my wife will find.
He'll be the modern type
and be called Rob or Simon or Mark.
He'll do the housework,
cook the meals,
do the washing up,
make the beds,
drive my daughter to school
and pick her up afterwards.

He won't have a temper like mine
or be subject to violent mood swings,
tantrums and depression.
Oh no, his mood will be calm and even.
He won't be pedantic or fuss like I have.
He'll be the perfect man,
a Socialist and a vegan,
the one I obviously am not,
though I thought we did all right for a bit.
I thought giving you a house, a kid,
a stable family life, was enough.
How wrong I was!

There will be a time for tears
This isn't it just yet.
It will be when I'm sitting
in my newly rented flat, on my own
and pondering every wrong turn,
hoping I can just turn back time
and undo all the things I've done.

Andy Botterill

CHANGING ROLLS

What happened to the Grannie's past -
Who used to sit with cat on lap?
Telling us tales about the past
Lots of knitting she used to do
Rock cakes and scones she'd bake
'Cut and come again cake' by the crate
She'd sit by the fire in her rocking chair
As quiet as a mouse
But if you look now
You'll find her down the Bingo
Just in time to hear her call *'House!'*

Sandra W Bridgeman

TOP MAN

Commissioning myself to write an unctuous birthday ode
Especially for someone of such intellectual mode,
I feel that plucking berries that as yet are harsh and crude
Before they're really mellow shows my lack of aptitude.

And with my lack of talent I have got to work quite hard
At ways and means of setting out a witty birthday card
But in this case I don't begrudge the effort and the ink
For Robin knows by now about the devious way I think.

For now I'm on my second pint I've sussed a double-cross
To write down 'quite sincerely' what I think of Robin Wass!
For he would know at once if I attempt to reminisce
About his looks, his talent, this would only take the . . .

So though I know that this great man would never really harm me (?)
I think it's best if I avoid being thought as coy and smarmy
About this man whose wit and charm, whose lofty erudition
Makes all his mates self-conscious of their lack of education.

They perch on stools around the bar, the local boring farts
And gape in awe at Robin's grasp of literature and arts.
And those on IPA - it's said all secretly aspire
To one day drinking lager (*Harp)* with status so much higher.

Quizmaster and numismatist, and father of a nation,
A raconteur, philosopher with such self-deprecation,
More bent to help the ignorant on Scotch and Exhibition
He leads us on to upward lawns of high sophistication.

To Robin Wass at sixty, let us toast in gratitude
He condescends so patiently with our ineptitude,
So no one at the Kittiwake would ever think it odd
To hear when Robin Wass comes in, the cry goes up . . .*Oh God!*

Patrick Brady

WAITING

The phone rings.
I want to hear a young man
with a gentle Galway accent
telling me that my grandchild has arrived
and that my daughter and their baby are just grand

I want to know
in intimate detail,
their looks
their sounds,
their soft milky smell

Catherine Bradbury

LIKE WINTER

I know why you stand so tall in my mind:
It's because I miss you;
And in missing you
The memory of your gentleness to me
Grows immeasurably

Like the grass in the garden without a mower,
Like the wind on the beach before a storm,,
Like a sunset.

And I know why you seem so infinitely gentle:
It's because you are not here:
Gone away without me
To where you have to go
Reluctantly

Like spring before the heat of summer,
Like a swallow with a nest in autumn
Like winter.

S M Hodgsden

THE WIND AND THE TREE

Moon glides because we love to
a tempting fate, this round

for she was young and danced
I'll ravish! I'll plunder! But no.

I hear the cornflakes
settle in their packet

I can see the flesh around
her mouth and eyes challenge

her carrot sequence
a riot really.

After getting out of bed
I was getting in the way of people

trains, progress
the ship had slipped its lunar passage

more than the bitter can swallow.
All this weathering!

isn't funny everywhere
so think on where a summer breeze

lingers, seeths, before
dismissingly fleeing trees' sad caress.

John Dillon

THE MEDALLION

Burning feet slower, rock hitting, stumbling,
Sun blistered eyelids, sand blasted skin,
Neck rubbed raw by the heavy medallion
Old Man With A Child, engraved on black silver.

The boy had encircled her neck with his gift
To keep her from danger, as they parted, he said.
She had nodded, smiling, disbelieving his promise.
A token to treasure, not for magic, but love.

Sand stretched ahead, endless wave after wave.
Heat shimmered, dancing, grain upon grain.
Where was the water, she remembered - beyond it?
Where men waited for words that would save them from death.

A sudden lightness, neck free from torture.
The medallion had fallen, its chain broken free.
She stopped, eyes on sand, watching it sinking.
Her talisman lost in the bottomless swamp.

She could now see the way. Ahead lay the water.
She would follow the detour, avoiding the trap.
And the soldiers would live, escaping disaster.
Because she has worn the medallion for him.

Eleanor Hamilton

SAIL AWAY

Slowly the ship left the harbour
its sails billowing like white clouds
Sun shining on the sea, glistening
broken only by the ships wake

You stood, tall and proud
as you bid a fond farewell
A tear came to my eyes as I watched you
So happy, so content

Soon the ship was out of sight of land
You turned, a smile came to your lips
I felt your hand reach out for mine
Your arms wrapped around me
the warmth of your breath
as we kissed, lingering

At that moment I was with you
as I will always be with you
as you will always be with me

Sheena Zeglicki

WOODWORM

Hiding in the wardrobe,
Breathing quietly,
Her husband opened up the door,
And asked me down for tea.

'Did you find the woodworm?'
He asked me, with a grin,
'None today, I'll look again,
Next time I pop in.'

Her husband's not the brightest spark,
He's simple to delude,
He thinks I search for woodworm,
Completely in the nude.

Jim Storr

ONE FINE DAY

A country walk on a summer's day
The air so fresh and scented
Then for no reason I could see
The air became demented

Scudding clouds cross
The windswept sky
Form many different patterns
Within the inner eye

Now and then a glimpse of sun
From behind the clouds is peeking
Sends down its rays like
Laser beams on programmed target seeking

If one finds you wherever you hide
And bathes you in its yolk
For one terrifying second
You think you'll disappear in smoke

Lightning flashes crack the sky
And thunder slaps the ears
And the smell of burning ozone
Brings your eyes to tears

All of a sudden the rain comes down
It's caught you on the hop
You've got no coat or brolly
And it's never going to stop

You finally reach shelter
The storm's not over yet
But there's one thing that you know for sure
You're very, very wet

James Valentine Sullivan

DAYDREAMS

Daydreams
A world far away,
A better place where children play,
Where flowers bloom,
All year long,
And babies dance in fields of corn.

Where dreamers dream,
And dreams come true;
Where I first fell in love with you,
Where summer never ends and happiness rules the world.
A simple moment with your favourite band
And you find that you are in Heaven, maybe.

But then I'm disturbed from this fantasy world,
And return doing work,
On the school white board.

Christina Faircloth

SOLITUDE

(People often mistake solitude for loneliness)

I was lonely as a mother,
Lonely as a wife
Completely lonely throughout my married life.
When the offspring grew, and flew the nest,
And my husband went to his long-earned rest -
I escaped into Solitude.

It was in this new realm,
I had time to see
Myself, in a strange new reality.

No more anxieties. No meddling in-laws,
Resentments, or fears
That had plagued me all those years.

No loneliness now -
Solitude wrapped me in a blanket of calm.
Self-appreciation became my balm.

M Fitzpatrick-Jones

REGRETS

You rue the words you've said, the deeds you've done.
How many times you've churned with memory-pangs,
through heat-of-the-moment incursions into the idiot zone:
so much on that minuscule moment of madness there hangs.
Impetuous throw-away brickbats hit home as intended,
but boomerang-like they return, with a message attached:
you cannot undo the offence, or deny you've offended
no deus ex machina miracle. You can't be snatched
and carried away to some fairytale lollipop land.
You must live with the knowledge of truth, that fact is fact.
Only faith in forgiveness may ease, maybe help understand
that self-remonstration is negative, fails to impact.
Now forward and upward are options you cannot but take
for you and your soul's and for everyone else's sake.

So start from the here and the now, looking sideways not back.
Take stock of the positive, leave what you've suffered behind.
Focus your sights on the present and get back on-track
and clear the decks of detritus and clear your mind.
Take joy in the good things around you and breathe-in fresh air;
admire the colours and smells, and the sights that you please.
Shut out all the cans of toxicity, darkness and care,
and dwell on the genuine pleasures that give you heart's ease.
Though you can't ignore the realities met with each day,
nor can you benumb all your faculties in a false dawn;
such negatives should not obscure your view of the way
you must go, if you hope to arrive at your goal, be reborn.
We none of us simply give up on our dutiful giving;
but nor must we give up the truth that our life is for living.

Adrian Brett

SCHOOL TRIP

Home - but now I'm back
at Mile End Underground
early evening rush hour
taking the Tube, then train
reversing out of Liverpool Street.

Late afternoon in Cambridge
reboarding before dashing down the road
to find the wrong coach.
Horse in field grabs sandwich
then looks for it in some boy's bag.

Lunch over and all that History
is making me hungry. We spend
the morning touring the Colleges.
Stations flash by: the train
arrives at Cambridge - it's
about to leave London.

'I shall have to bang
a few of you on the head.
You clots!' Where is everybody?
Glad I had breakfast -
must be time to go.

B Garfield

DEATH OF THE INNOCENTS

Silence hangs heavily in the room
Where twenty-six small coffins lay
Each containing the body of a child.

Outside amongst the debris and rubble
People sit weeping, praying, moaning
In an air heavy with the stench of grief.

Some sit numbly looking at the heap
Which once was the village school
That imploded with the earthquake's shock.

Blankness and despair are etched on faces
As they try to make sense of this tragedy
Which has befallen this Italian community.

David A Garside

WALES AWAKENING 'THE END OF AN EMPIRE'

In the land of poets, art and song,
the easel-mind lulls upon an empty canvas,
dry brushes with passionately exhausted hairs
hesitate with a nervous ponder.

Thoughts that file from a euphuistic - history
evolved to subdue the native of the day,
clarify the pretence of an Act euphemised,
and the migrant borne with a right of intolerance.

Age is a revealer.
The arsonist of truth, sows a signature of ashes,
amidst the bonfire, carried on angelic - winds,
Aneirin the witness, slips the flames.

Symptom is no healer.
A battle cry, high cords for harmonious years,
rhythm voices carry on drumming - winds,
the warrior Celt's march, for aria hymns.

A cure in her.
From a god-like hand, Bronwen draws breath,
emotions fold the mind, fingers mold the fears,
streaming eyes the screaming skies,
Christopher Williams flows reluctance tears.

And in defiance the archive groans
with poems, art and song,
released as whispers, amongst the ever drone
through the cultural bland, we seek our Inspirational Home.

Berwyn Barter

BEAUTY IN A SPIN

To be beautiful inside and out
Instils within the opposite sex,
Panic and self doubt
For one can be too beautiful to be discrete
Too alluring, too unique.

Too bold, too pretty
Too wise, too witty
Too beautiful, too sweet
Too charming, too complete.

Too scintillating, too entertaining
Too ideal, too surreal,
Too slim, too trim,
Too stunning, and I am perceived quite cunning.

Too caring, too sharing
Too sexy, too daring
Too genuine, too feminine,
Too good to be true
What the heck am I to do?
Too this - too that
I no longer know, where I'm at.

Being attractive can be a curse and a crime
Evoking insatiability so distinct and sublime.
The beautiful long to be accepted for who and not what they are,
Yearning to be on a general equal par.

And so to hell with equality, beauty is worth every dime
Love me or leave me for with my ass-et I'll climb
Alas, people are far from gracious and so unkind
I may be considered pretty, also dumb but at least I can rhyme.

M Barnett

MELODY DIVINE

Sunshine and roses
with a musical rhapsody,
Setting your feet a-tapping
enthralling you with
a melody so divine.

Ladies a-whirling
in beautiful gowns,
of colours of all array.
Twirling and twisting
with partners so proud
with a melody so divine.

The last waltz is playing,
partners are leaving,
under a moonlit sky,
With a thousand stars
shining down,
Leaving the melody so divine.

Jean Gill

PARADE OF HISTORY

Through the mists I see them
A parade of history
They march in my thoughts like soldiers
Onward to the sea
The famous men of Devon
Who sailed the seven seas
And made a nation's story
Carried on the freshening breeze.

The ships that sailed the world
The men of sword and steel
That travel the mighty oceans
With one hand on the ship's wheel
Raleigh, Drake and Hawkins
Upright men and true
Fought under England's banner
The only thing they knew.

They fought that this island
This jewel set in blue
Should always be its own master
To its own self be true
They fought for Queen and country
To uphold Britannia's rule
To free us from European shackles
And dictators oh so cruel.

They must now view with sorrow
All that the future has brought
Tied forever by a tunnel
To those with whom we fought
No longer a proud island
Just a place on a map
Where history is forgotten
As our strength Europe saps.

Margaret Gurney

OUR FAVOURITE SPOT

Remember our special picnic place?
That flat patch of grass by the tree by the stream
Where swans came looking for leftover scraps
But given the chance would have taken the lot.
Remember those summers so sultry and hot?
We choose to forget the ones that were not
Remember the laughter, the games and the fun
Planning the next time during that one.

Remember the red wine tied with a string
Placed in the water to chill from the start?
Always the first job when we arrived
Even if rain came we had something done
Remember our special picnic place?
How time after time we returned to the scene?
It would be nice to do it again
Alas it can only repeat as a dream
The place is still there but time has moved on
It was our place, a time once upon.

Terry Grimson

THE WHITE DOVE

I had a vision of a pure white bird
Soaring over land and sea
Singing a song I'd never heard
As it flew over me.

I asked why did it look so sad
As it flew over sea and sand
It said it's becoming harder each day
To find somewhere to land.

And I wondered why so many could not hear the song it sings
How I long to see the day when the white dove
Rests its weary wings.

It said what's come over mankind, some kind of strange disease
Why is it when he looks he very seldom sees
How do people listen, but they don't really hear
Why do they show hatred, makes my eyes fill with tears
How can he touch, but not really feel
What's happened to mankind, has he lost touch of what's real?

It then sang of peace, it sang of love as it flew so high above
Said, 'You can help me find somewhere to land - just reach out
                                            your hand.'
So why not reach out your heart today by holding out your hand
And together you can help this white dove find somewhere to land.

And I wondered why so many could not hear the song it sings
How I long to see the day when the white dove
Rests its weary wings.

Freddy Gates

THE EXILES

'And there was no more sea,' so wrote the seer,
An exile, far from friends and those he loved,
Held on the rocky isle of Patmos drear,
Yet like a rock his faith he held unmoved.

So through the ages have the exiles longed
For safe return across the boundless seas,
Slaves by the avarice of captors wronged,
Chained, branded, treated as commodities.

The Pilgrim Fathers, o'er the vast expanse
Of the great deep, though perilous their flight
From persecution, earnest, brave, in lands
Of the New World, sought to pursue the light.

And soldiers, sailors, airmen serving long
In regions far, with eager spirits yearned
For that glad day when, with a joyful song
To families and loved ones they returned.

Prisoners condemned, transported to strange climes,
Captives with meagre prospect of release,
And refugees made outcast, by the crimes
Of cruel dictators, dream of home and peace.

O ye who taste the fruits of liberty,
Forget not those who from the tyrant fly.
Look mercifully on the refugee,
Say, 'There but for the grace of God go I.'

John W Garland

SCARS

Scars,
Some we wear for all the world to see.
Scars,
Some we hide away from prying eyes.

Scars that we carry,
A silent burden to the soul.
Scars that we're married to
For the whole of our lives.

Scars to give, scars to receive,
Scars that heal, scars that bleed.

We've all been Children of a Scar,
We've all been Parents to a Scar.
Some take and make their pleasure
As the mistresses of grief who tend the graves
Of those who felt beyond hope and gave up
To fall victim to their own scars.

Some never recover from the scars of the heart
Others brush aside such memories with the cuff
Some dwell in a twilight of the scars of the mind
Others cope with openness to their disabilities,
Their bodies and souls at war for the injustice
And ridicule, that can pour from those more fortunate.
Scars within, scars without,
Scars that weep, scars that shout.

Richard Gould

SHE REMEMBERED

Never a stream ran so swift
As love stifled, stopped and dies,
Love depleted, rippled in ribbons
Reflected in continuous slivers of sky.
Running, twisting and turning
Far out of reach, those salted saline tears,
Drip and plop into the stream
Grey water mingled, skimming dragonflies.
Then to trickle through reflections
Dodging brackens, reeds and dogwood,
Growing down the streams' grassed sides
Brown newts waddle, warty skin noted
Tails swish water, suction fingers
Grasping the rocks, old shoe and pebbles.
Where her tears melt in shallow waters
A sudden stick comes flying over,
Splashing in the warm, musty water
Black Labrador bounding after,
Wetting her lonely figure back to time,
Shaking droplets cascade over her
Showered into reality by the dog.
Children laugh, adults shouting in the distance
Come here Rover, you bad boy . . .
Then she remembers, yes he was.

Susan Carole Gash-Roberts

beautiful yet threatening,
abyrinths of Helen's dreams
nd nameless dread
ecall.

ner stalker was, *between*
but without substance.
ense. Then came a spasm
soundly slept.

Breakfast and he seemed distant.
Tidying the bed, she raged, betrayed,
powerless at the unknowable:
hurling the soiled nightwear to the wash.

A restless night, flickering with shadows.
A cab arrives. In the silence, voices drift.
Below, father loads his luggage.
Inside, beauty bides with smiling threat.

Looking to the bedroom window,
he waves goodbye. Gone. Forever.
Menace and hurt possessed her.
Anguished, she returned to bed . . .

Weeping, she felt for the comfort of her doll.
John stirred to her touch.
Exhaustion then claimed her
as she drifted into night.

In the catharsis of deepening sleep
truth displaces fancy:
Gone is her father,
but gone, too, is her thief in the night.

Ron Hails

BRAVEHEART: WILLIAM WALLACE

At last . . .
'I understand the secret.'
The smell and taste of a misty dawn,
Before the sun has risen,
Before the night has gone.
New memories, stolen by the eyes.
In the silence, there's the prize.

Do you feel the passion in the anger?
The tears.
The baited breath in fires of death.
Coldness knows no emotion.
The severing sword, without compassion, the throat is cut.
Here lies the plot, the battle's roar.
Between the solitude of death,
Where beauty hides behind the cloth.
The pain and anger, the evil wrath, are blessed and burnt.

The flames are cold: against the burning hate.
The mouth is dry.
Fear takes hold the heart.
But inspired by faith, the cragged face knows love.
But what madness to keep score.
The arrow swift, the sharpened tip,
Pierced the heart once more.

Now . . .
When words are not enough.
The blooded sword and severed head.
Where now the battle's roar?

Now breathes the sweetened breath:
With words not heard before.
On bended knee you came,
From far beyond the call.
That your words have given nothing:
But in your eyes there lies the truth.
Slaves or freedom, love is in disguise.
With words unspoken, there is born the seed of deceit, in ashes.
The pierced heart is betrayed once more.
The betrothal cloth is stained with blood:
As each ragged scar and broken bone
Aches for home,
The unblooded ground.
The ghosts will have their revenge.
The legend will go before.
No spoken words, just prayers and dreams.
In love, there lies,
'The Braveheart.'
Held in the eyes of a child, a smile.
The ghost has called,
The cry is:
'Freedom!'
The bloodstained betrothal cloth becomes the flag.
The battle is won.

'The heart is free, have the courage to follow it.'

Nigel Gatiss

BACK STAB

There are 37 days until sunrise,
Night has descended like a friend
With daggers pointing.
Keeping both eyes firmly forward
As naïve flesh is exposed from behind.
In a world of non believers,
Enemies and allies converge as one.
Everyone has their price,
Even those held dear.
They can turn at any moment,
Scratching beneath your surface
With an incestuous heartbeat.
When the light falls dark, that is
When you are most vulnerable.
They attack in groups when you least expect;
When your guard is down
And when you're not even there.

Jondaniel Harris

UNSURE

Empty thoughts
I'm totally out of sorts
Unsure what to do
Unsure what to think
So unsure
I feel life's a chore
If only people really saw

They call me a bore
If only they knew that I'm so unsure
So quiet
So scared
In the back of my head I feel their glare
I wish they would ask me instead of stare
So unsure
Mind you, who knows what's round the corner
But I know one day that they will be one of my mourners.

Cheremane Hartery

CHAMPAGNE COCKTAIL

Strange elegance, limpidity of pleasure
Golden treasure, reflecting in salons and mirrors.
In the depth of a flute a few bubbles - remained, resisted
Traces, the memory of an exquisite soiree
An arm reached out, suited, guiding an elegant neck
A leg slipped thro' black sequins
A framed hand of cards - resting
A sheathed figure slips by, taffeta teasing

Exquisite glass, voluptuous lips
Sips, dips - colours dance
Figures glide thro' dusk-laden gardens
On glass-topped tables reflections shimmer
Evening shoes brush lawn carpets
The women pluck long stems, gather bouquets
Drink in the aromas, drown their lips
Their glasses full, the game faked,
The men play their cards, offer champagne like kisses
The gods have left the table
Bottles, like passwords circulating, lay abandoned
As proof, or souvenir, spectacular and secret.

Marilyn Hodgson

DEAR GRANCHA

As we are all sat here holding Nan in our numb arms,
Tears crashing onto floorboards
Trying hard not to scream and shout at God,
Why don't you walk in?

Why don't you sit down,
Let me buy you an orange and soda,
I'll bring you over a plate of ham sandwiches
And a sausage roll.

I don't think anyone here will mind
If you want to moan about your leg,
Or tell stories of when you worked on the railways,
Or boast about your children, grandchildren, great grandchildren.

Please walk in from the garden smelling of compost
Sit in your favourite chair, I'll make a cup of tea
And watch biscuit crumbs fall from your mouth
While you show me old photos.

Carly Hughes

WHAT WILL I BE?

Will I be a princess
Will I be a witch
Will I be famous
Will I be rich

Will I be clever
Will I be a fool
Will I be short
Will I be tall

Will I be poor
Will I be rich
Will I be famous
Will I be Kitsch

Will I be happy
Will I be sad
Will I be lucky
Will I be bad

Will I be weak
Will I be strong
Will I be right
Will I be wrong

You are lovely
and you will be fine
You are lovely
Just wait and see in time.

Sheree Rackham

THINKING

I am trying to think
What I can write

Nothing coming to me
Nothing that's right

That's why it's not coming
I am thinking

Looking around the room
At the flowers
At the wall

Still nothing coming

Ah, but wait a minute
Something has come

Letters
Words
Thought
Action by pen

So something
Did come
From nothing

Cynthia Osborne

A CORNISH DREAM!

Living in Cornwall is so peaceful,
So beautiful, so quiet,
Until the tourist season begins,
And then there starts the riot!

We sit in clover from September to May,
So lovely and serene,
But then the calendar is turned to June,
And we all feel a stifled scream.

We now know their indicated left, means right,
Of this there is no doubt,
As they travel round in circles,
Oh, what are they about?

Their shouts, 'We're 'ere,' vacating their cars,
Using other we cannot mention,
We try to be helpful, nay polite,
But this only increases the tension.

The local supermarket is the first place they go,
Shouting, 'Oy mum, this looks nice, I'll buy it,
I'm really considering that during these months,
I'd much prefer to diet!'

Cries of ''Ere Dad, where are ya?'
Makes us all look in disbelief,
But it's when the knotted hanky appears,
We all feel depressing grief.

''Ere mate, what's this sign say?' they bellow,
As devilment fills your face with glee,
When you're tempted to direct them round the bend,
That ends up in the sea!

Children screaming, litter everywhere,
Oh, good gracious what a din,
You would never think the British tourist,
Would have ever seen a bin.

Reading a book is a trying past time,
Best wait till you're safe in bed,
As trying to enjoy the next page,
A beach ball lands on your head!

At last the beaches are cleared of debris,
Finally you can walk there in peace and alone,
As it's time to shed a tear,
School's back! At least they've all gone home.

J L Novak

HIPPY MAN WITH MAGIC EYES

Put a seed in my head
That grows and blooms.
Dreams of peace and love
And all things good.
Karma man
Travelling down the lane.
Very good gardens
Bright and beautiful.
Flower glowing in the sun
Take my hand and float
Through the gardens.
Like smoke through trees
Herb in hand
Like a rainbow
So beautiful and free
Hippy man.

Robert Peckham

IF ONLY

Skinny-berlinky, long legs is all I want to be,
Not a frumpy, dumpy, ordinary mother of three.
I dieted,
Joined slimming clubs,
Exercised each day.
But somehow never managed to keep the fat away,
I've been told it does not matter
That I'm cuddly not fat.
But when I see the models,
I'd like to be like that,
So I'll carry on healthy eating
And maybe just one day
I will find out,
My fat has gone.
That it just slipped away.

Lyn Peacock-Sayers

A JOLLY JUGGLER

Washing's nearly finished, breakfast table's laid,
Homework's done and ready to go, packed lunches freshly made.
Three uniforms washed, pressed and aired, hang ready to be worn,
However did I spend my time before my kids were born?

Coffee's on, warm pastries out, fruit juice is in the jug,
Each child will sit in 'their own' place, and use their favourite mug.
Our 'Alpha male', in white bathrobe, will grunt and crash about,
'Who's moved my lap-top? Where is it? Will come his usual shout.

'It wasn't me, ask Naughty Nina, she's always the one.'
'That's so unfair, don't start on me Jo . . . tell her, Mum!'
'My tummy hurts, can't go to school, I think my leg's broken.'
The crafty one, our young son, plays his malingering token.

And so the chaos carries on, in a comfortable sort of way,
In spite of all the fuss that's made, they're ready for the day.
Now eight-thirty, first job's complete - my family out the door,
The cat's been fed and gone to bed, left paw prints on the floor.

I can't stop now, the mess will wait until my next 'home shift',
Procrastinate, or I'll be late, don't want to miss my lift!
Our morning smells still in the air, I close the door behind me,
In eight hours time, we'll all be back, what should I get for tea?

Umbrella up, briefcase in hand, food shopping on my mind,
Must think about my day ahead, not what I've left behind!
New sales figures I must chase, my greedy boss appease,
He doesn't know and wouldn't care of our domestic crises.

I love it though and wouldn't change my life for any other
The thrills and spills, this juggling act of working wife and mother!

Margaret Paxton

HOLDING ON

I sometimes feel like
I'm holding my breath.
Clinging to life.
Dismissive of death.

This hospital room
all white with tiles,
the aroma of antiseptic.
The nurses' smiles.

I'm cosy and warm
in my cocoon.
The world hovers on the edge
of my hospital room.

Still another day dawns.
I see the sun
and rejoice in the fact
of another day won.

I keep holding on.
I like cheating death.
Is that why I feel
like I'm holding my breath?

Maureen Reynolds

A Spider In The Bath

When the autumn leaves are falling
And people are weather installing
Then a great big spider sought refuge in my bath.
Now don't you laugh!
Fetch a duster quick
Then drop it over him does the trick.
I free him in the garden
And he quickly scuttles away
Threatening to return on the very next day.

Henry Rayner

FOOT PASSENGER

Go my love do what you do
If he could love you as I do
If he could take your hand
For a walk along the sand
When I miss you
Eyes brimming with tears
If he could weep like child
Who need mother's breast
Even h's much a money
And have some power
He couldn't smelt rose
Or to defer between thorn and flower
What kind of woman you're
Go to learn who is the real poor
Have you ever been in school?
Or passing your time
Near your swimming pool
Getting sunbathe!
You liked always to be cool

Hacene Rahmouni

FAT CATS

Look at the sea of angry faces
Frustration
Eyes wide open, but they do not see.

Bumping into each other
Hate you.
Your neighbour owns something you desire
A video? Hi-fi?
They are not brothers and sisters in love.
More like rival siblings
Who all clamber for the last slice of cake.
Cream around their faces.

Fat cats are the jealous kind.

Man hating man
He must be hating himself.
He does not understand himself.
His foe is his brother
Spit and scratch (like cats)
Fight to the death.

Fat cats fight the dirtiest.

Seen the underground lately?
Someone's under the wheels.
'Bloody inconvenience, I'll be late for the office.'
But who died?
Nobody asks.

Reading the newspapers come first.
Your mother, brother, father, sister?
Who cares?

Fat cats have the hardest hearts.

Someone whispered, 'Food is scarce.'
Watch them, scramble to the shops.

Ten loaves, twenty loaves
Won't they all go stale?
Can you eat all that?
It does not matter.
My brother can go hungry.

Fat cats are the greediest.

My hate runs so deep
Then so too my love
A two-sided coin
Decide which side to flip
And keep it that way.
We all have the choice.

Fat cats are the loneliest.

You know you have a body
But what about your soul?
You cannot buy a better one
You cannot steal your neighbours

If only they would see.

Fat cats could be purring.

Lindsey Susan Powell

FROM THE RANKS OF MEN

From the ranks of men children will come
Who were born for this time
From the ranks of men soldiers will come
As an army stands in line
From the ranks of men prophets will come
Who will tell of what God's decreed
From the ranks of men intercessors will come
Who will stand and intercede
From the ranks of men dreamers will come
With a vision for unity
From the ranks of men artists will come
And paint what the dreamers see
From the ranks of men singers will come
With a new song to sing
Their voices joined in unison
At the heralding of the king
From the ranks of men watchmen will come
Who will watch for each city and town
And as they patrol their gates and walls
The strongholds will come down
From the ranks of men each will come
From every tribe and nation
From the ranks of men at this time
A chosen generation
From the ranks of men a hope will come
For those who are down cast
Rise up and dance your light has come
Your time is here at last
From the ranks of men musicians will come
Whose music will pave the way
For us all to join as one
As we approach the coming day

From the ranks of men desire will come
A burning passionate flame
That will light the way of change for us
So that things are never the same
From the ranks of men they will come
Those who are right and true
From the ranks of men at this time
Will come people just like you

Carl Phillips

AGE

Why does every birthday
Reinforce the law of gravity?
And hair, receding from the head,
Now grow from every cavity?
It's nature's most vindictive,
Reprehensible depravity;
Experience could pave the way
For comfort, ease and fun.

But every single working part
Gets harder to maintain;
Now, where there once was colour
Only lighter shades remain,
And any small abuses
Bring ten times their weight in pain
As any careless damage now
Can never be undone.

Yet, if I had an offer
To become sixteen once more
With the same lack of perspective,
Or knowledge, as before
I'd only want to do it
If I knew I could be sure
I could return
When hope's succumb to reason had begun.

Gayna Florence Perry

SPHINX

Saucer-eyed sorceress,
Egyptian goddess,
Visions of a desert
Reflected in golden orbs.

Memories of worship
Ending in entombment.

Spirit rose and travelled to my hearth.
Now I kneel at this feline shrine
And praise the beauty that is Cat.

Val Spiers

WHEN THE WIND BLOWS

When the wind will blow
I'll go with the flow
Now I wish to be head of time
For years I've been slow
Lazy airs drift me here and there
Christmas desires for the snow
We have good days and bad
Trees stand before God and bow
Gust of wind knocks at my door
Moon wishes to enter, I will allow
Heart predicts, head refuses
Time seems to care for me now
God give me strength to stand
I cannot deny what I saw
I can't put a name to a face
What is his name? Call him now
Winds bring along the scent
The passion enhance my mind now
Traders purchase hearts often
Traitors are low life low
Now that I don't want it
Success chases me now
The word love inspires me
Let's organise the photo show
The ego might just accept
The passion land, if wind blow
Wind blows only in on one direction
What friends suggest, heart disallow
Permit, heart to select the path
The passion wind will blow

N Shahzadi Alam

When The Wind Blows

Blue lights shining through
The Guildhall stones
I walk with pace on the way home

I took a step back from my life today
Went to my youth, strong memories of school days
That's when the wind blows
Straight to the spine
Straight to my mind.

The gods testing my confidence?
Perhaps
It will not be broken for the remaining years
Even through deep tears.

Andrew Ryan

THE BEACH

As he sat upon the beach
The whole world seemed within his reach
Children playing in the sand
Older ones running as only they can.

Babies playing in great big hats
Mums and dads lying flat;
The smell of suntan all around
Everyone trying to get really brown.

Yachts racing out to sea
Seagulls soaring in the breeze
Tankers delivering loads of oil
Everyone hoping the sea won't spoil.

People looking for a spot
Aren't we humans a funny race?
Balls being kicked up and down
Loads of ice cream all around.

Young girls walking up and down
Wearing bikinis and a frown
Ticket collectors coming round
To make you pay for the chair you've found.

As the sun climbs high in the sky
Some small babies start to cry
The sun has reached its peak
It's time that they all went to sleep.

Beef burgers and chips smell everywhere
As people eat without a care
Why should they worry on a day like this?
It's a day you should not miss.

Cliffs gleaming in the midday light
You can even see the Isle of Wight
Powerboats racing in the waves
Children searching for shells in caves.

And as the day draws to an end
People say goodbye to friends;
Some wend their weary way
Others decide to stay.

He thought of all times gone by
Packed his things with a smile
Went off on his way
Glad he'd been here on this day.

K Rowe

CALL OF THE WILD

Amber, crimson, gold and tan
Where once 'twas shades of green
This natural turning of the leaves
Is such an awesome scene.

The xylem tissues, no more food
Unto the leaves provide
Thus giving the impression that
These mighty plants have died.

The trees so naked in the breeze
Skeletonised 'til spring
Their dormant season soon will end
When new life will begin.

The hardy annuals also die
They've given up their best
Now hibernating 'neath the soil
To start a time of rest.

Where we continually take our rest
Botanical rest is 'Fall'
There's ne'er the possibility of
Ignoring nature's call.

Colin Ross

THE TRAVELLER

So much of his life's berated,
His caravans in pastures seen,
His children, hungry, never sated,
His wife wanting herself to preen.
Cheap her clothing and at times old,
Patched here and there, a winsome tear,
Worn to a frazzle if truth were told;
Stolen from someone's line this gear.

Policemen the traveller dreads,
They'd as soon move the bastard on
Off the land with smelly skin 'eads
As see him to a prison gone.
Futile is the traveller's rage,
Grown old in life's pretentious war
He sees time wither on its stage
While slim hope's dangled from afar.

His life's a broken melody
Its quality at times so poor
At best confused to a degree
Locked in a barren, artless score.
His world wrecks itself by stages;
A poor ranger astride a nag
In the knacker's yard he rages,
His sad life turned into a student rag.

Why do good men no longer care?
Making an old gypsy beg bread,
Passers-by who just stand and stare
Whose slow feet drag on; not swift-led
To fulfil a traveller's need
Of a stout heart's so loving spell.
A lone horse, an unquiet steed
Is a vagrant traveller in a day's hell.

Angus Richmond

STORM IN A TEACUP

When I blew hard into my cup,
a vision did unfold,
of tiny ships and raging seas,
and sailors who were bold.

The briny spume soaked crack and pore,
as it merged with piercing rain,
fine timbers cracked as brave men screamed,
their bodies wracked with pain.

As mighty waves crashed over decks,
smashing masts and unfurled sails,
faint cries of grief could just be heard,
amidst the intense gales.

With huge waves breaking fore and aft,
the crews were filled with dread,
now focused on their fragile lives,
they mourned comrades who were dead.

Whilst vessels floundered on submerged rocks,
in waters that were deep,
my cup slipped gently from my hand,
as I awakened from my sleep.

L Idell

RAIN BIRDS

The rain touches me with cold sparks
Cold yet gentle as they fall off the backs of the birds
It covers the clouds coloured grey
And parts to form a bright blue sky peering through
With the birds that fly next to angels

The soft whiteness of the pure birds bring comfort and peace
As they glide with such care
Into the world of the non-understandable
Lifting those who fall, above the clouds with their vigour

I am dripping wet but I feel unperturbed and protected
I feel content in all that I am
Happy in myself
Alive to the world

The birds are singing a cheerful song
My heart is beating a dozen and nine
And my soul dances to its tune once more

Sharon Barnes

SUBMISSIONS INVITED
SOMETHING FOR EVERYONE

POETRY NOW 2003 - Any subject,
any style, any time.

WOMENSWORDS 2003 - Strictly women,
have your say the female way!

STRONGWORDS 2003 - Warning!
Opinionated and have strong views.
(Not for the faint-hearted)

All poems no longer than 30 lines.
Always welcome! No fee!
Cash Prizes to be won!

Mark your envelope (eg *Poetry Now) 2003*
Send to:
Forward Press Ltd
Remus House, Coltsfoot Drive,
Peterborough, PE2 9JX

OVER £10,000 POETRY PRIZES
TO BE WON!

Judging will take place in October 2003